A New Illustrated Rosary

—

JOHN

FAMILY PUBLICATIONS

OXFORD

The publication of this book has
been made possible through a kind
donation from two parishioners in
the Diocese of Northampton.

Introduction

> Beholding as in a mirror the glory of the Lord,
> we all are transformed into the same image,
> from glory to glory. (2 Cor 3:18)

'Contemplation is a gaze of faith, fixed on Jesus.'[1]
The Rosary is geared towards this gazing; its
focus is this intimate eye contact with the Lord.
With images from illuminated manuscripts acting
as icons, this is the principal aim of this prayer book:
to 'contemplate with Mary the face of Christ.'[2]

'Your face, Lord, do I seek' (Psalm 27:8). This face-
to-face transforms us. As St Paul puts it, 'beholding
the glory of the Lord' involves being 'transformed
into the same image.' This means being changed by
the One whose face we contemplate; it means being
changed into the One whose gaze meets ours in
these mysteries. This beholding entails becoming;
the outcome of this looking is likeness. Such is the
path of conversion traced by the Rosary.

Our eyes are openings, letting us out and others
in. They are the route that revelation takes. Looking
deeply means letting down our guard. What we pay
attention to has the potential to move our minds, to
motivate our decision-making and to drive forward
what we actually do   that is the grace of this great

---

[1] *Catechism of the Catholic Church*, 2715.
[2] John Paul II, *Rosarium Virginis Mariae*, 3.

prayer. We are converted by what catches our eye – that is what we hope for from the Rosary and why we are invited to mine its mysteries with 'generous eyes'.[3]

Just as the hub of each Hail Mary is the name of Jesus, so he is the centre of gravity of this 'exquisitely contemplative prayer'.[4] In his life, death and Resurrection the Lord Jesus traces the contours of true love. And he embodies it for our imitation. The Rosary's concluding prayer expresses the ultimate objective of these mysteries: 'that we may imitate what they contain and obtain what they promise.' Jesus himself is the One these meditations invite us to imitate. And Jesus is the One they promise we shall ultimately obtain.

May our minds and hearts be shaped by these mysteries as they steep us in the Gospel stories. May this evangelical prayer help us to sustain this eye contact with the Lord, always deepening our relationship with him. In this gazing may we be 'entranced by the beauty of the Redeemer.'[5] With our eyes fastened on him, may we gradually become what we behold.

Canon John Udris

---

[3] Ibid., 40.

[4] Ibid., 12.

[5] Ibid., 9.

At the beginning of the Rosary:
✠ Sign of the Cross
Apostles' Creed
One Our Father, three Hail Marys, one Glory Be

At the end of the Rosary:
Hail Holy Queen, Mother of Mercy,
hail, our life, our sweetness and our hope.
To thee do we cry, poor banished children of Eve;
To thee do we send up our sighs, mourning and weeping
in this vale of tears.
Turn then, most gracious advocate, thine eyes of mercy
toward us and after this our exile show unto us the
blessed fruit of thy womb, Jesus.
O clement, O loving, O sweet Virgin Mary!

℣. Pray for us, O Holy Mother of God.
℟. That we may be made worthy of the promises of Christ.

Let us pray:
O God, whose only-begotten Son, by his life, death and
resurrection, has purchased for us the rewards of eternal
life; grant, we beseech you, that meditating on these
Mysteries of the most holy Rosary of the Blessed Virgin
Mary, we may both imitate what they contain, and obtain
what they promise, through the same Christ our Lord.
Amen.

℣. Most Sacred Heart of Jesus ℟. Have mercy on us.

℣. Immaculate Heart of Mary ℟. Pray for us.

Prayers

The Sign of the Cross

In the name of the Father
and of the Son
and of the Holy Spirit.
Amen.

The Apostles' Creed

I believe in God, the Father almighty,
Creator of heaven and earth,
and in Jesus Christ, his only Son,
our Lord,
who was conceived
by the Holy Spirit,
born of the Virgin Mary,
suffered under Pontius Pilate,
was crucified, died and was buried;
he descended into hell;
on the third day he rose again
from the dead;
he ascended into heaven,
and is seated at the right hand
of God the Father almighty;
from there he will come to judge
the living and the dead.
I believe in the Holy Spirit,
the holy catholic Church,
the communion of saints,
the forgiveness of sins,
the resurrection of the body,
and life everlasting. Amen.

The Our Father

Our Father, who art in heaven,
hallowed be thy name.
Thy kingdom come.
Thy will be done on earth, as it is in heaven.
Give us this day our daily bread,
and forgive us our trespasses,
as we forgive those who trespass against us,
and lead us not into temptation,
but deliver us from evil.
Amen.

The Hail Mary

Hail, Mary, full of grace, the Lord is with thee;
blessed art thou among women,
and blessed is the fruit of thy womb, Jesus.
Holy Mary, Mother of God,
Pray of us sinners, now and at the hour of our death.
Amen.

The Glory be

Glory be to the Father, and to the Son, and to the Holy Spirit,
As it was in the beginning, is now and ever shall be,
world without end.
Amen.

The Fatima prayer (at the end of each decade)

O my Jesus,
forgive us our sins,
save us from the fires of hell.
Lead all souls to heaven,
especially those in most need of thy mercy.

Joyful Mysteries

Introduction

The Biblical word shared by each of the joyful mysteries is 'behold'. It is in the astonishing invitation the angel makes to Mary, as well as the first wonderful word of her consent (Lk 1:31 and 38); it is there in the Magnificat when Mary summons her cousin to see how all generations will call her blessed (Lk 1:48); it is in the song of the angelic host to the shepherds to go and see the birth of the Saviour (Lk 2:10); it is in the prophecy of Simeon to Mary at his presentation to perceive the mysterious destiny of her child (Lk 2:34); it even begins Mary's appeal to her son to see the distress he has caused when she finds him teaching in the Temple (Lk 2:48). 'Behold' is used whenever there is something so amazing that it demands our wholehearted attention. It means 'look!', 'see!', 'sit up and take notice!' All this requires generosity. This is the hallmark of the characters in these mysteries. And in a beautiful way they all embody the outcome of this generosity: joy.

Behold, the handmaid of the Lord;
be it done to me according to your word.
(Lk 1:38)

The Annunciation of the Lord

Meditation

In this scene the angel Gabriel appears to be genuflecting.
In conceiving Christ within her, Mary has become the
tabernacle of God here on earth. The angel is wearing a
dalmatic, the vestment of a deacon. It symbolises the servant
he is, and which Mary has now so beautifully become. But
the centre of the whole scene is Gabriel's finger. Pointing
towards Mary it expresses the fact that of all women she
is the one who has been chosen for this unheard-of role.
Her flesh will play host to the holy of holies. She has been
singled out for this unique responsibility. Mary gazes on that
finger with fear and trembling. The angel assures her that
'full of grace' she can fulfil this incredible calling.

Imitate: Our Lady's listening

Obtain: The joy that comes from answering God's call

Prayer

℣. Mary, Full of Grace ℟. Pray for us.

Our Father, ten Hail Marys, Glory be.

Blessed is she who believed,
for there will be a fulfillment of the things
which have been spoken to her from the Lord!
(Lk 1:45)

The Visitation of the Blessed Virgin Mary

Meditation

Look at all the buildings in this picture: a castle, a church, a windmill, a house. They point to, but pale into insignificance before, the habitations that Mary and Elizabeth have both themselves become. The Holy Spirit has made of them the dwelling place of grace. They embrace the holy in each other. There is no higher destiny of the human body than to become the home of God himself. The hill behind Mary evokes the hill country of Judah across which she has hurried to greet her cousin. Just like the Ark of the Covenant had travelled those same hills in the Old Testament. John leaps in Elizabeth's womb. Just as King David had once danced before the Ark. Both are bursting with joy because of the imminent arrival of our Saviour.

Imitate: Mary's believing

Obtain: The grace of being inhabited by God himself

℣. Mary, Ark of the Covenant   ℟. Pray for us.

Our Father, ten Hail Marys, Glory be.

She brought forth her firstborn son,
she wrapped him in bands of cloth,
and laid him in a feeding trough.
(Lk 2:7)

The Nativity of Our Lord

Meditation

Angels are everywhere in this scene. They are busy with the humblest tasks: one carries a cushion, another a towel, one is carrying water, while another is stoking a fire. They symbolise what has happened with the birth of this child: heaven has come to earth. Earthly realities, even the most menial, are filled with meaning and significance. These angels are emblems of God's providence. They help to illustrate that what seemed to be the wrong place at the wrong time – a smelly stable at midnight – was actually just the right place at just the right time in God's plan. Meanwhile Joseph scratches his beard in wonder at what God is up to, and in amazement at his own place in that plan.

Imitate: Joseph's awe and wonder

Obtain: The joy of being instrumental in God's providential plan

℘

Prayer

℣. Mary, Cause of our Joy   ℞. Pray for us

Our Father, ten Hail Marys, Glory be.

Behold, this child is set for the falling
and the rising of many.

(Lk 2:34)

The Presentation of the Child Jesus in the Temple

Meditation

Look where they have laid the Child Jesus. There's no mistaking where he is being placed by Mary and Simeon in this scene: on the altar. Simeon prophesies. He has set eyes on the Saviour. He knows the destiny and the very identity of this child is sacrifice. And that Mary's own martyrdom will be somehow bound up in all this. Simeon says to her, 'A sword shall pierce your own soul too.' Both Joseph and Simeon appear to be marvelling at Mary as she hands over her son. They are amazed at this love 'that lays upon the altar the dearest and the best', as the popular hymn puts it. They recognise the quality of fairest love in this letting-go.

Imitate: Mary's surrender

Obtain: Serenity in the midst of suffering

Prayer

℣. Mary, Mother of Fairest Love   ℟. Pray for us.

Our Father, ten Hail Marys, Glory be.

"Didn't you know that I must be in my Father's house?"
… his mother kept all these sayings in her heart.

(Lk 2:49,51)

The Finding of the Child Jesus in the Temple

Meditation

Mary's entrance in this scene appears to be an intrusion. She has obviously interrupted something important. The scribes and doctors are busy double-checking their books. They are excited. They don't want to be disturbed. Jesus is already overturning their ideas at the age of twelve. He is already accomplishing his mission: moving minds, changing hearts, opening up new horizons. Maybe Mary begins to realise that her Son is already about his Father's business. With each one of these mysteries Mary had something to treasure in her heart and turn over in her mind. And we have too.

Imitate: Mary's treasuring in her heart

Obtain: True wisdom

∽

Prayer

℣. Mary, Seat of Wisdom   ℞. Pray for us.

Our Father, ten Hail Marys, Glory be.

Luminous Mysteries

Introduction

Light reveals. It uncovers as it illuminates. Even a little goes a long way. Each of these mysteries of light exposes the identity of Jesus. They let us into the secret of his personality. They illumine the purpose of his life as the unique revelation of God. Light reflects. Making clear his mission as they do, at the same time these mysteries clarify our own. He who said, 'I am the light of the world', also said, 'You are the light of the world.' Each of these particular episodes is an epiphany, not just of the Lord, but of our own calling. Each contains enlightenment for our self-understanding. Light transforms its surroundings. This was the chief effect of Christ's ministry. The same is meant to be true of our lives. Moreover, it is the nature of light to change things into itself. Whatever it shines on, itself becomes shiny, radiant, luminous. This is the ultimate effect of our relationship with the Lord: we are to be transformed into him, to glow with his glory, to become 'light in the Lord' (Eph 5:8).

This is my beloved Son,
with whom I am well pleased.
(Mt 3:17)

The Baptism of Jesus in the Jordan

Meditation

The waters of the River Jordan in which Jesus kneels are translucent, we can clearly see all the fish. Likewise the water gushing out of heaven is transparent, we can clearly see the Holy Spirit. Similarly this scene makes clear the mystery of Christ's true identity. Grace gives us eyes to see through to who he is: the Father's beloved Son, on whom his love is abundantly poured out. His nakedness looks back to his birth and forward to his death and to the accomplishment of his mission. The angel waits to invest him in the dalmatic of a servant. The purpose of this ordination is crystal clear – to serve. We see reflected in this icon our own baptism day when we were all made sharers in the same mission.

Imitate: Jesus' standing under the torrent of God's grace

Obtain: To live in the grace of our baptism day

Prayer

℣. Mary, Mother of Divine Grace   ℟. Pray for us.

Our Father, ten Hail Marys, Glory be.

Jesus' mother was there.
(Jn 2:1)

The Wedding Feast at Cana

Meditation

'Jesus' mother was there.' That's how that story begins.
That's what made all the difference that day. The mother
of Jesus 'was there' at his first miracle, just as she would be
there at his final glorification on Calvary. Being there is
what the best mothers do best. The figure of Mary in this
picture seems to be pushing Jesus forward. She presents the
predicament to her son. She trusts him to transform the
situation. 'Do whatever he tells you,' she says to the steward.
And the willingness of the steward to fill those empty jars
with water was all that was needed. Hers is still the best
advice. Whenever we do what the Lord tells us his hand is
outstretched over us and he will let his glory be seen
(Jn 2:11).

Imitate: The willingness to do whatever Jesus tells us

Obtain: The revelation of his glory in our lives

℘

Prayer

℣. Mary, Mother of Hope   ℟. Pray for us.

Our Father, ten Hail Marys, Glory be.

You are the light of the world.
A city located on a hill cannot be hidden.

(Mt 5:14)

The Proclamation of the Kingdom of God

Meditation

Here Jesus is preaching his famous Sermon on the Mount. We can see that the mount on which he is sitting is his pulpit. At this point he is teaching them to pray the Our Father. At the heart of this prayer, the cornerstone of each decade of the Rosary, are the words 'Thy kingdom come!' How is that prayer answered? 'The Kingdom of God is within you' (Lk 17:21). Our lives are to be a proclamation of that kingdom. Did those disciples understand as they sat there on that mount that they were themselves to be the city built on a hill top which cannot be hidden? And that they were called to be the Beatitudes that were making their hearts burn that day. By means of those Beatitudes our lives become the location of God's kingdom.

Imitate: The Beatitudes

Obtain: The Kingdom of heaven

℘

Prayer

℣. Mary, Poor in Spirit and Pure in Heart ℞. Pray for us.

Our Father, ten Hail Marys, Glory be.

As he was praying,
the appearance of his face was altered,
and his clothing became white and dazzling.

(Lk 9:29)

The Transfiguration of the Lord

Meditation

It was 'as he was praying' that Jesus' clothes began to shimmer and his face began to shine. And the two people who appear with him on the mountain top that day knew very well that this is the effect of prayer. Moses, after he had prayed, covered his face with a cloth, because his encounter with God on the mountain left him glowing. Elijah, when he was exhausted, prayed, again on a mountain, and the still small voice he heard made him wrap himself in his cloak knowing he was in the presence of God. Prayer is our face-to-face with the Father. It's how we glow with God's own glory. In this decade of the Rosary let us resolve once more to climb the mountain of prayer each day, in order to encounter there the one in whose presence we are transfigured and whose afterglow in our good works we are called to show.

Imitate: The prayer of Moses, Elijah and Jesus

Obtain: The transfiguration of our lives

Prayer

℣. Mary, Morning Star   ℞. Pray for us.

Our Father, ten Hail Marys, Glory be.

As they were eating, Jesus took bread,
gave thanks for it, and broke it.
He gave to the disciples, and said,
"Take, eat; this is my body."

(Mt 26:26)

The Institution of the Eucharist

Meditation

This is not only the last supper they will share, it's the last sermon they will hear. Taking and breaking bread Jesus anticipates being taken later that evening and being broken the following day on the Cross. What will happen to this bread and wine will happen to him. It is the supreme revelation of who he is and what he has come to do – like light, to shed itself. But as he holds up the host he is inviting his disciples to see in it their own reflection too. 'Your own mystery lies here upon this table … be what you behold and receive what you are' (St Augustine, Sermon 272). The most fitting response to the Holy Eucharist is both adoration and imitation. Because Christ's Body is who we are called to be.

Imitate: The bread that is broken and the cup that is poured

Obtain: Our transformation into Jesus

Prayer

℣. Mary, Woman of the Eucharist   ℞. Pray for us.

Our Father, ten Hail Marys, Glory be.

Sorrowful Mysteries

Introduction

The *Stabat Mater* is a beautiful ancient hymn for the feast of Our Lady of Sorrows. Its title comes from the Gospel's description of Mary 'standing near the cross of Jesus' (Jn 19:25). It's a prayer addressed to Mary seeking with her a share in Christ's passion. It contains the following verse:

> Let me to my latest breath,
> in my body bear the death,
> of that dying Son of thine.

This prayer poignantly evokes the experience of St Paul. He described himself as 'always carrying in the body the death of the Lord Jesus, that the life of Jesus may also be revealed in our body' (2 Cor 4:10). This is the grace sought for in these sorrowful mysteries. It means identifying ourselves with all the Lord went through. But more than this, it involves an invitation to walk that way too. In these mysteries Christ embodies for us a love that gives itself away. The blood, sweat and tears they contain are the body language of the self-giving that has saved the world. Here Mary teaches us that 'standing near' her Son means far more than physical proximity. It's a daily decision by which we must play our part, like Mary, in the story of salvation.

Put the sword into its sheath.
The cup which the Father has given me,
shall I not surely drink it?

(Jn 18:11)

The Agony of Christ in the Garden

Meditation

In this scene consider the chalice and the sword. One is gilded with angelic light, while the other lies without lustre in the shadows. They symbolise two contrasting tactics. The sword represents our instinctive way of operating. We take things into our own hands; we reach for our own resources; we rush to our own defence. This will be Peter's automatic reaction. But, as Jesus has told him once before, 'the way you think is not God's way but man's' (Mt 16:23). The chalice on the other hand represents a very different strategy. To choose to stay vulnerable; to rely on unseen yet unassailable resources; to abandon ourselves into the Father's hands. In this mystery we seek to make our own the prayer which paves the way for all God wants to accomplish: 'not my will, but yours be done.'

Imitate: The obedience of Jesus

Obtain: The fulfillment of the Father's will

Prayer

℣. Mary, Woman of Obedience   ℟. Pray for us.

Our Father, ten Hail Marys, Glory be.

Pilate had Jesus flogged,
and delivered to be crucified.
(Mt 27:26)

The Scourging at the Pillar

Meditation

Look at the eye contact in this image. The gaze of violator and victim meet. What does the soldier see in the eyes of Jesus? Certainly not what he expects to find. No anger; no bitterness; no desire to take revenge. The Lord looks at him with eyes that are wells of unfathomable love; eyes that are filled with pity for the man who in flogging him is in fact inflicting wounds upon himself. In this scene the one who is bound is the one who is truly free. Because he does not answer back in kind, but with something altogether different. He teaches us the love that absorbs evil, turning the other cheek. This is the love on which the true axis of history turns. And it has the power to turn us too into the people he has redeemed us to be.

Imitate: Jesus' fortitude in the face of suffering

Obtain: The ability to love our enemies

&

Prayer

℣. Mary, Mirror of Justice   ℟. Pray for us.

Our Father, ten Hail Marys, Glory be.

They braided a crown of thorns
and put it on his head.
(Mt 27:29)

The Crowning with Thorns

Meditation

In this scene there is a striking symmetry between the crossed and bound hands of Christ and the crossed reeds of those who press the crown of thorns into place. It is the signature of love used by those who write letters to their loved ones. These last acts of Jesus, including his receiving of this cruel crown, bear the signature of God's love for us in spite of everything, even our rejection of him. As the soldiers use their rods to force down this crown, Christ appears as a fulcrum who is actually levering them up. He takes our humiliation of him and makes it the means of raising us up. He takes the worst we can do to him and makes it the best he can do for us.

Imitate: Jesus' gentle strength

Obtain: The undoing and defeat of evil

༝

Prayer

℣. Mary, Mother of Consolation   ℞. Pray for us.

Our Father, ten Hail Marys, Glory be.

As they came out, they found a man of Cyrene, Simon by name, and they compelled him to go with them, that he might carry his cross.

(Mt 27:32)

The Carrying of the Cross

Meditation

Count up all the weapons being wielded in this picture. They are symbols of power and influence. Yet the real weapon is the one Christ is carrying. And the real power resides in the burden Simon is singled out to help him bear. The privilege of helping Jesus carry his Cross was the supreme moment of Simon's life. This deed would shape his destiny. It shows us our own: to share in the work of salvation. Jesus gazes intently, as if outstaring the suffering with perfect love, his eyes on the prize of our Redemption. With Simon let us fix our eyes on him, 'looking to Jesus the author and perfecter of our faith, who for the joy that was set before him endured the cross' (Heb 12:2).

Imitate: Simon's carrying the Cross of Jesus

Obtain: The grace to play our part in the story of salvation

Prayer

℣. Our Lady of Perpetual Succour ℟. Pray for us.

Our Father, ten Hail Marys, Glory be.

Jesus, crying with a loud voice, said,
"Father, into your hands I commit my spirit!"
Having said this, he breathed his last.

(Lk 23:46)

The Crucifixion of Our Lord

Meditation

The whole world is gathered at this redeeming of the whole world: the good and the bad, the high and the low, the interested and the indifferent, his friends and his enemies. Even the stars in the heavens have come out to watch. The skull is Adam's. As if to say that all humanity is being redeemed. That the paradise that was lost is about to be regained. And the key to that paradise is the Cross. The Cross towers above the chaos saying something new is being created. The shape of the Cross and the shape of Christ's body both trace the letter 'T'. It is the first letter of the word 'trust', which is the raw material of this re-making of history. 'Trust triggers miracles' (St Thérèse of Lisieux, Letter 129). The greatest miracle of all is proof of the truth of this.

Imitate: The trust of Jesus Christ

Obtain: The gift of salvation

Prayer

℣. Our Lady of Sorrows   ℟. Pray for us.

Our Father, ten Hail Marys, Glory be.

Glorious Mysteries

Introduction

The final prayer of each decade of the Rosary points to the final purpose of each episode on which we are meditating. Moreover, it points to the final purpose of our lives: 'Glory be…' In the Scriptures God's glory is in the first place how he reveals himself. In the Exodus from Egypt, the people saw his glory in the pillar of cloud that led them by day and the pillar of fire that led them by night. In all the previous mysteries of the Rosary this glory has been gradually growing brighter. In these glorious mysteries that glory is at its most dazzling. Here we contemplate the clearest and most radiant revelations of the glory of the Lord. But this glory has its counterpart in our lives. Being converted by what we contemplate is how we give glory to the Lord. More than that, by God's great mercy, this glory becomes our deepest identity and eternal destiny. 'From glory to glory' (2 Cor 3:18) is the story of our salvation.

❧

Awake, you who sleep,
arise from the dead,
and Christ will shine on you.
(Eph 5:14)

The Resurrection of the Lord

Meditation

Contrast the eyes of Christ in this icon with the eyes of those guarding his tomb. Their eyes are tight-shut while his are wide-open. They are sleeping through the greatest event that has ever taken place on the face of the earth. Their closed eyes match the sealed tomb they were meant to be watching. While the open eyes of the Risen Lord match the tomb that is now open and empty. These eyes of Christ engage us: 'Don't be afraid. I am the first and the last, and the Living one. I was dead, and behold, I am alive forevermore' (Rev 1:17-18). Overtaken by this supreme revelation of God's love we quiver in wonder. 'This is the Lord's doing. It is marvellous in our eyes' (Psalm 118:23).

Imitate: Our Lord's all-conquering love

Obtain: The grace to overcome every obstacle with Him

❧

Prayer

℣. Mary, Mother of the Risen Lord   ℟. Pray for us.

Our Father, ten Hail Marys, Glory be.

As they were looking, he was taken up,
and a cloud received him out of their sight.
(Ac 1:9)

The Ascension of Jesus into Heaven

Meditation

Their eyes are all fixed on the Lord as he ascends to the home he has won for us. This mystery lifts our gaze and makes us look above and beyond. It trains our eyes on our true end; it asks us how intent we are on our eternal future. This ability to gaze into glory makes possible the kind of discernment by which our decisions can be judged correctly: 'Is this helping me heavenwards or not?', 'Am I focused on short-term gain or everlasting advantage?' Moreover, this mystery seeks to encourage us in our task of helping others to reach their heavenly destiny as God's sons and daughters. And of inspiring them to aspire to those glorious heights for which we all have been created and redeemed.

Imitate: The Apostles' gazing into glory

Obtain: The grace to attain our true end

Prayer

℣. Mary, Gate of Heaven   ℟. Pray for us.

Our Father, ten Hail Marys, Glory be.

They were all filled with the Holy Spirit.
(Ac 2:4)

The Descent of the Holy Spirit

Meditation

Look at the two characters seated in the foreground of this scene. One is reading an open book. Perhaps he is reading the Prophets who foretold this great day. The other, the one Mary's eyes are focused upon, holds out his open hands. As if he knows these prophecies are now coming true. Does he sense that he, and all the others in that Upper Room are now themselves becoming that open book, that word of God to the world? As St Paul puts it, 'you are a letter of Christ … written not with ink, but with the Spirit of the living God; not in tablets of stone, but in tablets that are hearts of flesh' (2 Cor 3:3). This is the supreme effect of being filled with the Holy Spirit.

Imitate: The openness of the Apostles

Obtain: The grace to be God's living word to the world

ॐ

Prayer

℣. Mary, Spouse of the Holy Spirit   ℟. Pray for us.

Our Father, ten Hail Marys, Glory be.

For he who is mighty has done great things for me.
Holy is his name.

(Lk 1:49)

FOURTH GLORIOUS MYSTERY

The Assumption of the Blessed Virgin Mary

Meditation

'Holy is his name!' These words from Mary's Magnificat are the equivalent of ones in the Lord's own prayer: 'hallowed be thy name'. 'Hallowing' or glorifying God's name means living in such a way as to make God known and loved, to magnify his reputation. In this scene we witness Mary's body worn out from a lifetime spent doing just that. Lying there at the end of her days she teaches us that there is no greater achievement than that our body has been an ambassador for God's greater glory. Mary's example makes us cry out in our turn 'holy is his name' as we consider the one whose whole being was always busy glorifying God. Her body and soul, now assumed into heaven, invite us to be busy doing the same.

Imitate: Mary's glorifying God's name

Obtain: The resurrection of our body

Prayer

℣. Mary, Queen Assumed into Heaven   ℟. Pray for us.

Our Father, ten Hail Marys, Glory be.

A great sign was seen in heaven:
a woman clothed with the sun,
and the moon under her feet,
and on her head a crown of twelve stars.
(Rev 12:1)

The Crowning of Our Lady Queen of Heaven and the Glory of All the Saints

Meditation

This last image, and the mystery it invites us to contemplate, takes us back to the very first. Only this time it's not Gabriel, but God himself who greets Mary. She bows her head to receive her reward for the fulfillment of that role she had once bowed her head to accept. Her hands are joined in the way they were at her Annunciation, in the way we have seen throughout these icons. Those praying hands express intent, purposefulness. Her fingers convey the consistent direction of her life – Godwards. Mary was completely focused on fulfilling the mission God had in mind for her. Looking carefully we can see that both God and Mary are smiling. There is no greater happiness than to have done what we were meant to do; there is no greater glory than to have been the saints God meant us to be.

Imitate: Mary's faithfulness

Obtain: Our crowning glory, eternal life

Prayer

℣. Mary, Queen of all Saints   ℟. Pray for us.

Our Father, ten Hail Marys, Glory be.

published by
Family Publications
Denis Riches House, 66 Sandford Lane
Kennington, Oxford, OX1 5RP
www.familypublications.co.uk

printed in England
through s|s|media ltd

Art credits

Cover: © Bibliothèque municipale de Chambéry, Ms 4, fol 9, Cliché Arkhenum

Page 1: © Bibliothèque municipale de Clermont-Ferrand, Ms 69, fol 416, Cliché CNRS-IRHT

Page 2: © Bibliothèque municipale de Tours, Ms 2104, fol 131v, Cliché CNRS-IRHT

Page 8: © Bibliothèque municipale d'Evreux, Ms lat 100, fol 19v, Cliché Stéphane Vuillemin

Page 10: © Fonds bibliothèque Méjanes, Aix en Provence,
Ms 16 (Rés. D. 495), fol 53, Cliché CNRS-IRHT

Page 12: © Photo Médiathèque de l'Agglomération Troyenne, Ms 3713, fol 43v,
Cliché Pascal Jacquinot

Page 14: © Bibliothèque municipale de Tours, Ms 217, fol 5, Cliché CNRS-IRHT

Page 16: © Bibliothèque municipale de Toulouse, Ms 2842, fol 69, Cliché CNRS-IRHT

Page 18: © Livre d'heures en "dialecte des Pays-bas" flamand XVe siècle, F.M 22, Collection
Musée de Sologne (Romorantin) – Fonds Emile Martin

Page 20: © Bibliothèque municipale d'Avignon, Ms 138, fol 53v, Cliché CNRS-IRHT

Page 22: © Bibliothèque municipale d'Avignon, Ms 121, fol 46, Cliché CNRS-IRHT

Page 24: © Bibliothèque municipale de Cambrai, Ms 189, fol 15, Cliché CNRS-IRHT

Page 26: © Angers, Bibl. mun., Rés. SA3390, fol 38v / CNRS-IRHT, base Enluminures

Page 28: © Bibliothèque municipale de Châteauroux, Ms 2, fol 249, Cliché CNRS-IRHT

Page 30: © Bibliothèque municipale de Châlons-en-Champagne, Ms 336, fol 22,
Cliché CNRS-IRHT

Page 32: © Collections Bibliothèque municipale de Rouen, Liber 142, fol 14,
Photographie Thierry Ascencio-Parvy

Page 34: © Bibliothèque municipale de Besançon, Ms 69, fol 28, Cliché CNRS-IRHT

Page 36: © Bibliothèque municipale d'Orléans, Ms 144, fol 84, Cliché CNRS-IRHT

Page 38: © Collection des silos, Maison du livre et de l'affiche, ville de Chaumont,
Ms 34, fol 29, Cliché CNRS-IRHT

Page 40: © Bibliothèque Mazarine, Paris, Ms 412, fol 150, 6 bis v, Cliché CNRS-IRHT

Page 42: © Bibliothèque municipale d'Evreux, Ms lat 99, fol 89v, Cliché Stéphane Vuillemin

Page 44: © Fonds bibliothèque Méjanes, Aix en Provence,
Ms 11 (Rés. ms. 35), fol 393, Cliché CNRS-IRHT

Page 46: © Bibliothèque municipale de Besançon, Ms 54, fol 18v, Cliché CNRS-IRHT

Page 48: © Bibliothèque municipale de Moulins, Ms 1, fol 342v, Cliché CNRS-IRHT

Page 50: © Bibliothèque municipale de Clermont-Ferrand, Ms 84, fol 97, Cliché CNRS-IRHT

Page 52: © Bibliothèque municipale de Valenciennes, Ms 122, fol 27v, Photo Thomas Douvry

Page 54: © Bibliothèque municipale de Limoges, Ms 2, fol 173v, Cliché CNRS-IRHT